What They Will Say

poems by

Jake Young

Finishing Line Press
Georgetown, Kentucky

What They Will Say

Copyright © 2021 by Jake Young
ISBN 978-1-64662-429-4 First Edition
All rights reserved under International and Pan-American Copyright Conventions. No part of this book may be reproduced in any manner whatsoever without written permission from the publisher, except in the case of brief quotations embodied in critical articles and reviews.

ACKNOWLEDGMENTS

Much gratitude to SALT for publishing "My brother explains" and "This morning, lying in bed;" to *Ponder Review* for publishing "I hike into the mountains;" and to *Lucky Jefferson* for publishing "The oldest maze."

Publisher: Leah Huete de Maines
Editor: Christen Kincaid
Cover Art: Jake Young
Author Photo: Jake Young
Cover Design: Elizabeth Maines McCleavy

Order online: www.finishinglinepress.com
also available on amazon.com

Author inquiries and mail orders:
Finishing Line Press
PO Box 1626
Georgetown, Kentucky 40324
USA

Table of Contents

Corn tassels shake in the wind 1
Stories from Ash Avenue 2
Monica tells me 3
Listening to Terrence Hayes 4
At Daisen-in 5
The brewer's family 6
My father says 7
My brother explains 8
The oldest maze 9
On the Philosopher's Path 10
Suffering 11
Rakushisha 12
At Mussel Fork 13
The morning Charlie didn't make it home 14
I hike into the mountains 15
Scholarship 16
There is structure 17
What They Say 18
A woman in a long, blue skirt 19
Meditation on Desire 20
On the windowsill 21
This morning 22
Affliction 23
Below the highway 25
What Remains 26
Reconstructed images 27
When the typhoon hits 28
From this distance 29
A train rocks along 30

for Dorianne and Joe

Corn tassels shake in the wind, while Japanese beetles eat their way into the husks. Scotch bonnets dot the edge of the field. Along the gravel road that borders the farm, people pass by in dust-covered pickups, wave with a finger, country nice, the stars and bars flapping in the wind.

Stories from Ash Avenue

I.
Q lived in a rundown house beside my apartment in Raleigh, but sometimes she disappeared for months on end. She was built like a fourteen-year-old boy, and came and went as she pleased. When she was in town, she DJ'd at Neptune's, my favorite dive bar. I ran into Q occasionally when she stopped by my neighbor next door, who, besides working as a professional photographer for children's sporting events, also sold cocaine.

II.
His hookup was a 350-pound black man everyone called Big D, except to his face, when he was referred to as just D. When I met Big D for the first time, I was a graduate student at North Carolina State. I told him I taught English Composition at the University as a graduate TA, and after that he always called me The Professor.

III.
I spent most of my time on Ashe Avenue outside on the fire escape. I'd sit on the cement steps, listening to music, or reading a book, a joint in my hand, and a half-drunk beer at my feet. I cut stencils out there—an open book, and the word "Read" that I spray-painted in front of the library; two hands holding iron bars in front of the prison. I had my own mural on a side street not far from there, but it was painted over shortly before I moved.

Monica tells me it's not either/or—

instead, she insists, it's both/and.

You can be whole and broken, hateful

and compassionate, the world is full

of such discrepancies and paradoxes.

The sun is always both rising and setting,

the tide always rising and receding,

we are always both living and dying.

The week before she died of a heart attack

outside the library, an unexpected but

inevitable event, Monica helped me realize

I can both perpetuate systemic racism

even as I fight against it. Even now, I hear

her voice both here and not here.

Listening to Terrence Hayes read from his new book on the radio in the car, I wonder what it means that I feel safe enough to ignore brutality. Lost in thought, I remember hearing that my father had been heckled at a reading during the Vietnam War; he was asked how he could write about nature after the bomb had been dropped, children were starving, and young men were being sent off to die? "I can't think of a better time," my father replied.

At Daisen-in

As I gaze at the rippling sand in the garden of swept stones, I feel as if I'm staring into the ocean. My mother tells me the garden is named "View of the Great Sea." My father says the monks here have been sweeping the garden in the same way for 500 years. A black carpenter ant crawls along the wooden steps of the temple, feasting on the same Japanese cypress that has fed its kind for generations.

The brewer's family has been making sake in Kyoto since 1726. He pours us clear, aromatic sakes, and cloudy rice wine that's sweet and nutty. He is the fifteenth generation of brewers, he tells us. His young daughter cries, and his wife crosses the tasting room to hold her. The brewer smiles, nods their way, and says "sixteenth generation."

My father says he doesn't like to backtrack, and even though the café we are trying to find is just a block-and-a-half the way we'd come, he'd rather keep moving forward. My brother quotes the Buddha, and tells our father not to be afraid to reminisce. We laugh, turn against the flow of the crowd, and continue back the way we came.

My brother explains that there are different kinds of infinity—countable infinities, like the endless string of whole numbers, and larger, uncountable infinities, like the limitless fractions between two integers. Words are countably infinite, but each word is uncountably infinite; I can imagine the unceasing invention of new words, each with a different meaning in every context. Looking out the window at the pastel houses that speed past as we drive towards a horizon we can never reach, my brother says, there are infinite other infinities, but those are complex.

The oldest maze we've discovered is 5,000 years old. The maze is a form found in nature, of wilderness domesticated, derived perhaps from our own intestines, our brain. My brother loved mazes as a child. He finished stacks of them, and every Halloween our parents took us to a corn maze at the pumpkin patch north of town. I once followed him through a dense maze, and at the end of it we came to a pool of enormous carp. We fed them breadcrumbs, and as a mass of writhing fish broke the surface, it sounded as if they were laughing.

On the Philosopher's Path

Everywhere we go, I notice creeping wire vine growing up the trunks of trees and along temple walls, its flat green buttons tattooing whatever it can reach.

I keep thinking I've seen it before, tasted it in the kitchen once when Chef brought some in by accident with the lettuce and herbs he'd harvested from his farm. Leaving the temple in the woods with the Buddha's footprint, returning to the Philosopher's Path, I pull off a glossy leaf from one of the mats of wire vine, snap it in half, and hold it to my nose.

It smells of sugar snap peas and cucumber. I set it on my tongue, and chew. I tell my family the monks used to eat this in hard times—my father jokes, they also used it as a diuretic. I wonder how they prepared it. The food of poverty, of famine, needs very little. My great-grandmother loved mustard greens; she'd send my father out to gather them from vacant lots, the way she'd done as a child growing up in Texas. In West Virginia, where my great-grandfather was a coalminer, like his father before him, salad meant a bowl full of miner's lettuce.

The food of the poor is ingenuity; you can find it growing anywhere. The world is full of bitter herbs—and they will nourish you, just sprinkle them with a little salt.

Suffering

I stayed with a friend at his father's cottage in the south of France. The cottage had no doors, the wallpaper had been torn away, and the walls had been painted over with a hallucinatory mosaic of swirling color. Later, I learned that the cabin had once been a gorgeous home. My friend's father, years ago, had been in a car wreck and a young girl had died. A father himself, he could not forgive himself the death of this child. Lost in grief, he withdrew into isolation, and tore the place apart room by room. What does it mean to call something damaged? After all, no one can ever recover from having lived.

Rakushisha

I.

Persimmons litter the ground after the storm. Awash in transience, we all become food for crows and ants.

II.

The night before the persimmon harvest, a great storm knocked all of the fruit to the ground. Mukai Kyorai, who owned the trees, had lost everything, which freed him to turn his hut into a modest temple, write poems, and abandon his dreams of wealth.

III.

A wasp burrows into the soft flesh of a persimmon in the abandoned orchard.

IV.

Black ants search the gravel for dead insects; cicada nymphs burrow into the sand to molt; spiders lie in wait in their webs.

V.

A stone is free of desire, not caring if it's flung into the pond, or left in place, not caring that it's a stone. Mukai Kyorai says, be like that stone.

At Mussel Fork

Once pried from the depths of imagination,
a name will cling to its referent the way a drowning man
holds on to hope. An hour past Pecan Valley,
there's a sign for Musselfork, a town with a stream
named for its abundance of freshwater mussels, though
I'm sure the stream had other names before
settlers came to eat the mussels they found there.
They turned the shells into buttons,
or ground them into temper for pottery.
The town is gone now, just a few old buildings
at the end of a dirt road, though the mussels remain
along the banks of the stream.
They filter the muddy water for plankton,
those microscopic alchemists
converting sunlight into air,
not unlike the towering pecan trees
that capture and release my breath
as their roots search for water. The pecans
and the mussels offer themselves
transformed in the darkness of their shells.
If I held them in the cupped palms of my hands
I could believe they were magic.
If I named them, I'd call them brother.

The morning Charlie didn't make it home, I rose early from the couch and left in the first light of the New Year. As the rest of the house continued to sleep, doctors picked fragments of bone out of Charlie's eyes. Three years later, addicted to pills, Charlie died the first time he stuck a needle in his arm. My head still rings with last night's wine.

I hike into the mountains, along a path beside a temple, its wooden doors drawn shut, past a sign I cannot read, a book, *The Ethnography of Rhythm*, in hand. Birds sing in the early morning light. There's meaning in pattern, not words, I think to myself. I whistle, and the birds sing back while I compose poems to them. Fat drops from last night's rain fall from leaves when the wind rustles; spiderwebs stretched between strands of grass wrap around my calves; and the birds continue to sing as I wander, a foreigner. When I reach the mountain top it's 6 AM, and a monk rings the morning bell for prayers.

Scholarship
> *The willingness to use our minds is what erodes our minds.*
> —Gary Young, "In the woods, hunting mushrooms"

Looking for a scrap of paper, I find a note I'd written months before: "The first poems were abstractions, proto-concepts, and therefore had to be interpreted." The word "Therefore" is abbreviated with three dots that form a triangle, the way I learned to build a proof one summer as a child when I took a class on logic.

There is structure to a finely written essay,
to the heart of a hummingbird, the feathers
of owls, the way heat rises and clouds move,
each song, every dance, social inequality,
political organizations, the history of sports,
synecdoche and syndicates, a bouquet
of flowers, a pair of socks, a spider's web,
to galaxies and time, to the entire universe,
but is there any structure to the present,
to eternal becoming, or like the number zero, is it
a concept or a symbol that contains only emptiness?

What They Say

Her poem about her boyfriend overdosing on heroin wasn't working. She was frustrated, grappling with sentimentality. "Tell me the story again," her professor said. She'd been drinking the night he died; he called her at a party; she was the last person to talk to him; but she had blacked out, and doesn't remember the call. "They say I said, 'I love you.'" "That's a great line," her teacher said, "write that down," and she did.

A broadside of the poem hangs in the pressroom where my father teaches. For weeks now that line keeps coming back to me, and the memory of the last time someone told me, "I love you." A girl and a boy in their early twenties were sitting on the sidewalk. They wore brown overalls with the legs rolled up, and had drawn on them in Sharpie—the anarchist A, swirling doodles, song lyrics, a dandelion. I was helping a professor move into a new apartment. The kids asked if we needed a hand, but we only had one last box to carry. The girl said it as I was walking away, "Love you," she called out after us, sincere yet cavalier, the way you might send off a close friend who has come to visit, whom you hope you will see again soon.

The weather is getting colder, and I wonder where those kids are now. Who can know how we will be remembered, or by who, if we'll even be remembered at all, and if we are remembered, what they will say we said?

A woman in a long, blue skirt rides her bike along a rice field. One hand steadies the bike, while the other holds an umbrella that shields her from the sun.

Meditation on Desire

Blue fingers of flame below the teakettle dance with the grace of an anemone. The day has ended, and now is a time for small desires. I desire tea and dark chocolate sprinkled with sea salt. Does an anemone desire that a crab move just close enough? Does the crab desire plankton, or the plankton light? How far down does desire go? Do molecules desire a specific shape? I know that the blue flame takes its shape upon combustion to allow the release of gas and the escape of heat, that it must do this to burn. Perhaps that's all desire is, a preferred way of being.

On the windowsill in the kitchen, my father dried wishbones. My brother and I would brace the splayed bones between forefinger and thumb and pull—whoever broke away the larger piece got to make a wish. I used to desire my own pleasure, but as I've aged, I now prefer to be desired, as I've learned that to please another is itself a pleasure. On the radio, a woman says that the clitoris is shaped like a wishbone. It is not the last pea at the tip of the pod; it is the shape of a wish, of pleasure waiting to break open.

This morning, lying in bed, I heard the same birdcall that echoed through the forest yesterday. When I opened my eyes, the room was dim, no birds could be heard, but there was the slow rumble of boiling water, and soon the house smelled of coffee. Though we cannot see the threads, *what was* pulls on *what will be*. Stuck in the present, how could I know that the clouds blown in yesterday would gather to drop rain on the roof this morning, or that the birds I heard will drink from the drops still resting on the leaves of the loquat?

Affliction

1.
There are things I like
about being sick.
People who never feel
sorry, feel sorry for you.
I enjoy their pity. I enjoy hot tea
and soft blankets, and the excuse
to do nothing,
to leave what needs to be
done for later; even the feeling
of weakness, faintness of breath
and body tingles. I like to imagine
what goes on within me:
my cells seeking a key,
the right shape to unlock
the virus replicating.
Thread through the eye
of a needle. A photon
through the atmosphere.
Whatever can get through
eventually gets through.
This destruction
I feel, a violence
we know as fever
and phlegm. Like any war,
there are traces left behind
in the rubble, biological scars
etched into our DNA.
What I like best is the comfort
of knowing that I can't
prevent what's already been
set in motion. Even this will pass.

2.
I once attacked the walnut tree
in front of my father's studio,
curious to see the sap.
The soft white flesh peeled away
so easily by the hammer's claw.
My father yelled, enraged.
The scab and scar, mark
of transformation.
The differences are what
a body notices.
When I feel heavy in my chest
but light in my bones,
almost high, even
my mind works differently,
absent minded, as if
in this state I am
somehow unaware of everything
except my body.

Below the highway, rice patties stretch to the base of the mountain. An irrigation pond lies in the distance, and nestled behind it, a graveyard grows with every season.

What Remains

Last week I dreamed of my grandfather. He stopped by to tell me something, but I can't remember what. All I can recall is that he looked good for a dead man, old but no longer frail. It was the first time I'd seen him since he'd died, though I think of him often when I dress for work and cinch one of his ties around my neck.

Reconstructed images show the statues of the Buddha's guardian demons were once painted blue, their hair a fiery red, their garments adorned like fine embroidery. At a museum in San Francisco, I saw an exhibit on ancient Egyptian and Greek statues, and they, too, had originally been painted in vibrant colors. Though the bright hues on the wooden columns here have long since faded, I can still depict the faint outline of the Buddha, swirling clouds, and a radiant lotus that a monk points out with a flashlight. Each column was made from the trunk of a single tree, the Greek influence clear, brought to Japan by way of India after Alexander the Great's conquests nearly 1700 years ago. This is how we will be remembered: increases in CO2, nitrogen, and phosphate levels, an abundance of technofossils, and the bones of chickens heaped in landfills.

When the typhoon hits, the banks of the Kamo River overflow where just yesterday we had ridden bikes, and the very edge of the riverbank where we had sat to enjoy a beer after our ride has eroded, washed away, the clear mountain runoff brackish and brown now with debris. Disaster follows my family, hand in hand with luck.

From this distance, the needle-like leaves of the cypress and the star-shaped leaves of the maples cannot be separated, their indistinguishable constellations moving in unison with the breeze. Wild bees search the sand for a mate, and climb the small dunes raked in the garden. Wings beat, and the line I had in my mind is gone. No matter, whatever I might have said, the ancients have already said it better.

A train rocks along the tracks. Rice patties ripple and wave.

Jake Young is the author of the poetry collection *American Oak* (Main Street Rag, 2018), and the essay collection *True Terroir* (Brandenburg Press, 2019). He received his MFA from North Carolina State University and his PhD from the University of Missouri. Much of his critical work focuses on the craft and theory of poetry and translation, and the intersections of food, drink, and literature. He is a Certified Specialist of Wine through the Society of Wine Educators, with over a decade of experience in the food and beverage industry. Jake was an artist-in-residence at Djerassi Resident Artist Program in 2014, where he was awarded The John D. and Susan P. Diekman Fellowship, and in 2018 he received the William Peden Teaching Prize in Creative Writing from the University of Missouri. He also serves as the poetry editor for the *Chicago Quarterly Review*.